WALTZING

TO MARJORIE COTTON

D.W.D.

Text: © Copyright Reserved, Proprietors: Retusa Pty Ltd
Illustrations: © Desmond Digby, 1970

First published in 1970 by William Collins, Sydney
This edition first published in 1987 by William Collins, Sydney
Typeset by Savage Typesetters,
Printed and bound by Dai Nippon Printing Co. (Hong Kong) Ltd.

National Library of Australia
Cataloguing-in-Publication data:

Paterson, A.B. (Andrew Barton), 1864-1941
Waltzing Matilda.

ISBN 0 00 662697 1.
1. Children's poetry, Australian. I. Digby, Desmond,
1933-   .II. Title. (Series: Fontana picture lions).

821'.2

WALTZING MATILDA

Poem by
A. B. Paterson

Illustrations by
Desmond Digby

Fontana Picture Lions
POCKET EDITION
COLLINS AUSTRALIA

Oh! There once was a swagman camped in a billabong,

Under the shade of a Coolabah tree;

And he sang as he looked at his old billy boiling,
"Who'll come a-waltzing Matilda with me?"

Who'll come a-waltzing Matilda, my darling,
Who'll come a-waltzing Matilda with me?
Waltzing Matilda and leading a water-bag—
Who'll come a-waltzing Matilda with me?

Down came a jumbuck to drink at the water-hole,

Up jumped the swagman and grabbed him in glee;

And he sang as he stowed him away in his tucker-bag,
"You'll come a-waltzing Matilda with me!"

Who'll come a-waltzing Matilda, my darling,
Who'll come a-waltzing Matilda with me?
Waltzing Matilda and leading a water-bag—
Who'll come a-waltzing Matilda with me?

Down came the Squatter a-riding his thoroughbred;

Down came Policemen — one,

two

and three.

"Whose is the jumbuck you've got in your tucker-bag?

You'll come a-waltzing Matilda with me.''

Who'll come a-waltzing Matilda, my darling,
Who'll come a-waltzing Matilda with me?
Waltzing Matilda and leading a water-bag—
Who'll come a-waltzing Matilda with me?

But the swagman, he up and he jumped in the water-hole,

Drowning himself by the Coolabah tree;

And his ghost may be heard as it sings in the billabong,

"Who'll come a-waltzing Matilda with me?"

GLOSSARY

BILLABONG: A backwater from an inland river, sometimes returning to it and sometimes ending in sand. Except in flood times it is usually a dried-up channel containing a series of pools or waterholes.

BILLY: A cylindrical tin pot with a lid and a wire handle used as a bushman's kettle.

COOLABAH TREE: A species of Eucalyptus, *E. microtheca,* common in the Australian inland where it grows along watercourses.

JUMBUCK: A sheep. From an Aboriginal word, the original meaning of which is obscure.

SQUATTER: Originally applied to a person who placed himself on public land without a licence, it was extended to describe a pastoralist who rented large tracts of Crown land for grazing and later to one who held his sheep run as freehold.

SWAGMAN: A man who, carrying his personal possessions in a bundle or SWAG, travels on foot in the country in search of casual or seasonal employment. A tramp.

WALTZING MATILDA: Carrying a swag; possibly a corruption of 'walking matilda'. 'Matilda' was a type of swag where the clothes and personal belongings were wrapped in a long blanket roll and tied towards each end like a Christmas cracker. It was carried around the neck with the loose ends falling down each side in front, one end clasped by the arm.